on earth as it is

Mikey Swanberg

on earth as it is

Mikey Swanberg

on earth as it is ©2021 by **Mikey Swanberg**. Published in the United States by Vegetarian Alcoholic Poetry. Not one part of this work may be reproduced without expressed written consent from the author. For more information, please write V.A. Poetry, 643 South 2nd Street, Milwaukee, WI 53204

Cover art by Esther Y. Kim

In this world
we walk on the roof of hell
gazing at flowers

Kobayashi Issa
        (Translated by Robert Hass)

I am a full grown man
I will lay lay lay
In the grass
In the grass
All day

Matthew Houck

on earth as it is

the tax havens
will soon be underwater
which in business
means bad
but in scuba diving sort
of means
you're in business

on earth as it is

the tax havens
will soon be underwater
which in business
means bad
but in scuba diving sort
of means
you're in business

on earth as it is

in the mega facility
where I last got medicated
powder for my undercarriage
shipped in two days

a robot explodes a can
of bear repelling spray

which it turns out
repels humans
in about the same way

on earth as it is

in the mega facility
where I last got medicated
powder for my undercarriage
shipped in two days

a robot explodes a can
of bear repelling spray

which it turns out
repels humans
in about the same way

on earth as it is

a human heart is found
on a plane   which leads
one flight attendant to ask

does anyone know whose heart this is

on earth as it is

a human heart is found
on a plane   which leads
one flight attendant to ask

does anyone know whose heart this is

on earth as it is

the world economic forum is held
in country known for chocolate
& minding its own business

which in business means
not minding if the money
you mind was stolen
by the nazis

on earth as it is

the world economic forum is held
in country known for chocolate &
minding its own business

which in business means
not minding if the money
you mind was stolen
by the nazis

on earth as it is

when announcing the newer new phone
the tech giant reminds us
that our old   now crummy phone
can be used as a flashlight
in the coming climate disasters

they suggest a 12 dollar
tool which charges
as you crank it

on earth as it is

when announcing the newer new phone
the tech giant reminds us
that our old   now crummy phone
can be used as a flashlight
in the coming climate disasters

they suggest a 12 dollar
tool which charges
as you crank it

on earth as it is

we charge as you crank it

on earth as it is

we charge as you crank it

on earth as it is

the swamps are filled
with bright orange signs

yes   the gators are frozen stiff
but no   the gators did not die

on earth as it is

the swamps are filled
with bright orange signs

yes   the gators are frozen stiff
but no   the gators did not die

on earth as it is

we watch a video of someone
pouring a large beer from Applebee's
into the smaller size beer from Applebee's
& all that is left is a single sip

on twitter Applebee's finally responds
to let the poster know
that they poured it wrong

on earth as it is

we watch a video of someone
pouring a large beer from Applebee's into
the smaller size beer from Applebee's
& all that is left is a single sip

on twitter Applebee's finally responds
to let the poster know
that they poured it wrong

on earth as it is

the gender reveal bomb
rigged in the desert
does exactly what it must
& explodes

the damage all told
is 182 square kilometers burned
8 million in losses to announce
the arrival of another boy

on earth as it is

the gender reveal bomb rigged
in the desert
does exactly what it must
& explodes

the damage all told
is 182 square kilometers burned
8 million in losses to announce
the arrival of another boy

on earth as it is

the phone pings to let me know
that if I buy a gift card
to the movies   I will earn
a special gift

I buy the gift card for myself
& in a few moments
the gift for buying the gift card

an additional   smaller gift card
is delivered to my inbox with a little ding

on earth as it is

the phone pings to let me know
that if I buy a gift card
to the movies   I will earn
a special gift

I buy the gift card for myself
& in a few moments
the gift for buying the gift card

an additional   smaller gift card
is delivered to my inbox with a little ding

on earth as it is

our come comes out
in the wash
is washed away
by a sweet blue soup
we pour into the machine
we made to ease
these needs

on earth as it is

our come comes out
in the wash
is washed away
by a sweet blue soup we
pour into the machine we
made to ease
these needs

on earth as it is

we get auto corrected incorrectly
we type   *I cannot talk*
right now   I am in the middle
of a snow fury

on earth as it is

we get auto corrected incorrectly
we say   *I cannot talk*
right now   I am in the middle of
a snow fury

on earth as it is

we sometimes kiss
like we never came out
of the sea   we see
one another clearly
& refuse to close
even the smallest seam

on earth as it is

we sometimes kiss like
we never came out
of the sea   we see
one another clearly
& refuse to close
even the smallest seam

on earth as it is

we play a game
where we are ruthless
train magnates
a few miles from the church
named after ruthless
train magnates

on earth as it is

we play a game
where we are ruthless
 train magnates
a few miles from the church
named after ruthless
train magnates

on earth as it is

in the disaster movie we watch
from our faux leather reclining
amc stubs premiere a - list seats

the animals look up from the lake's edge
& are the first to flee

which reminds us we haven't heard
birds in a week

on earth as it is

in the disaster movie we watch
from our faux leather reclining
amc stubs premiere a - list seats

the animals look up from the lake's edge
& are the first to flee

which reminds us we haven't heard
birds in a week

on earth as it is

the boys are fooling around again
by the docks & then the boys are in the water
& the lifeguard says they are in trouble
but really they are just in love & can't say it

which on earth as it is is a different lick of trouble

on earth as it is

the boys are fooling around again
by the docks & then the boys are in the water
& the lifeguard says they are in trouble
but really they are just in love & can't say it

which on earth as it is is a different lick of trouble

on earth as it is

we pluck the single hair from the mole
& two grow back in its place
after the two   four
& after the four   eight

we are in love with this doubling
but things simply can't go on this way

on earth as it is

we pluck the single hair from the mole
& two grow back in its place
after the two   four
& after the four   eight

we are in love with this doubling
but things simply can't go on this way

on earth as it is

we learn that technically Crocs are edible
but that the team at Crocs
does not suggest you eat them

on another site
a one line post says

boil them first

on earth as it is

we learn that technically Crocs are edible
but that the team at Crocs
does not suggest you eat them

on another site
a one line post says

boil them first

on earth as it is

it is not all bad
a friend comes by with fresh flowers
& then at work a colleague comes by
with a mechanical flower that dances
when the sunlight
hits his little solar belly

on earth as it is

it is not all bad
a friend comes by with fresh flowers
& then at work a colleague comes by
with a mechanical flower that dances
when the sunlight
hits his little solar belly

on earth as it is

I take a short walk
to get coffee & to feel
the sun on my big body

there's no life waiting
beyond this one   loves
no chores

more important
than keeping kind
no matter what

on earth as it is

I take a short walk
to get coffee & to feel
the sun on my big body

there's no life waiting
beyond this one   loves
no chores

more important
than keeping kind
no matter what

on earth as it is

the marine corps sniper
is accidentally a poet
when he tells the young snipers
not worry to about being the bushes
& to instead become
the space between the bushes

on earth as it is

the marine corps sniper
is accidentally a poet
when he tells the young snipers
not worry to about being the bushes
& to instead become
the space between the bushes

on earth as it is

we remind a coworker not to honeymoon
on the beaches near the scene of an active genocide

we suggest the beaches near the scene
of a decades old genocide   which are also quite lovely

···

on earth as it is

we remind a coworker not to honeymoon
on the beaches near the scene of an active genocide

we suggest instead the beaches near the scene
of a decades old genocide   which are also quite lovely

on earth as it is

we see through the neighbor's large windows
that another mass shooting has occurred

we were otherwise enjoying the day
but now we are on earth as it is
again

on earth as it is

we see through the neighbor's large windows
that another mass shooting has occurred

we were otherwise enjoying the day
but now we are on earth as it is
again

on earth as it is

the ladybug finds the light
glowing off of pornhub
in the otherwise dark home

aren't our houses on fire
our step-bros at home

on earth as it is

the ladybug finds the light
glowing off of pornhub
in the otherwise dark home

aren't our houses on fire
our step-bros at home

on earth as it is

the newspaper says
we need about 10 hugs a day
& that 6 seconds would be good
but that 20 seconds is even better

we think *yeah that seems about right*

on earth as it is

the newspaper says
we need about 10 hugs a day
& that 6 seconds would be good
but that 20 seconds is even better

we think *yeah that seems about right*

on earth as it is

our gmail's predictive text
displays the end of our poem
in light gray letters
before we even type them

I am sorry   the poet says
I'm running a little late

on earth as it is

our gmail's predictive text
displays the end of our poem
in light gray letters
before we even type them

I am sorry   the poet says
I'm running a little late

on earth as it is

we drive along the highway named after the ocean

which we can see from our rental car
does look like a thousand diamonds
strewn across a blue blanket
just like incubus said it would

huh   we say   I'll be damned

on earth as it is

we drive along the highway named after the ocean

which we can see from our rental car
does look like a thousand diamonds
strewn across a blue blanket
just like incubus said it would

huh   we say   I'll be damned

on earth as it is

this is it   we say
as a stranger comes
into our homes

bathroom is here
bedroom bedroom
kitchen obviously

so yeah   that's about it

on earth as it is

this is it   we say
as a stranger comes
into our homes

bathroom is here
bedroom bedroom
kitchen obviously

so yeah   that's about it

on earth as it is

we buy succulents
& then google

how to care for succulents
browning succulents

how to tell if your succulent has died
& finally

where downtown to buy cacti

on earth as it is

we buy succulents
& then google

how to care for succulents
browning succulents

how to tell if your succulent has died
& finally

where downtown to buy cacti

on earth as it is
        (by Franklin K.R. Cline)

i call mikey from my car after i buy a new york times
on a rainy sunday morning

hes in kentucky he sounds happy and floaty like mikey

ill see him soon

mikey and i played a game once where you had big long arms
and you punched each other

i would punch a lot of people in real life but not mikey

anyway its rainy again today im getting ready to go see brian
and have tacos i just had therapy i just finished THE BEATLES'
SECOND ALBUM
and won $1000 on the suns

on earth as it is
        (by Franklin K.R. Cline)

it rains and we get wet and then we go eat food or make food
we put gas in our cars

on earth as it is we love our friends we love love
we are earnest now we have eschewed irony

on earth as it is

in the amazon we learn
first that fish are singing
& then that these songs
are a type of fighting

on amazon I order
glow in the dark dracula fangs
because it is that time
of year again

on earth as it is

in the amazon we learn
first that fish are singing
& then that these songs
are a type of fighting

on amazon I order
glow in the dark dracula fangs
because it is that time
of year again

on earth as it is

a couple divorces
& we are asked to pick sides
though we abstain

only to find years later
we accidently did

because we are still following
the couple's celebrity cat online

on earth as it is

a couple divorces
& we are asked to pick sides
though we abstain

only to find years later
we accidently did

because we are still following
the couple's celebrity cat online

on earth as it is

a bumble bee lands
on our finger as fat & happy
as an engagement ring

we weren't planning on marrying
but we find ourselves
again opening to anything

on earth as it is

a bumble bee lands
on our finger as fat & happy
as an engagement ring

we weren't planning on marrying
but we find ourselves
again opening to anything

on earth as it is

we mute our headphones
to hear the political conversation
happening at the bar in the Whole Foods
about the rich & horrible candidate

only to realize we are hearing the ad
of the rich & horrible candidate

& the people in the bar are talking
about homemade pizza dough

on earth as it is

we mute our headphones
to hear the political conversation
happening at the bar in the Whole Foods
about the rich & horrible candidate

only to realize we are hearing the ad
of the rich & horrible candidate

& the people in the bar are talking
about homemade pizza dough

on earth as it is

a man asks the concierge
to help him find an article
called *96 ways to chill out*

which appears on the cover of the magazine
in the lobby   but which he cannot find
within the pages themselves

you see he says   *it isn't in here*
I'm going to sue the magazine

on earth as it is

a man asks the concierge
to help him find an article
called *96 ways to chill out*

which appears on the cover of the magazine
in the lobby   but which he cannot find
within the pages themselves

you see he says   *it isn't in here*
I'm going to sue the magazine

on earth as it is

some of the things I like best
about myself I bought

my boots   my bright red coat
but other things   like tying a cherry

stem into a knot
with my tongue

I learned the old fashioned way
by getting used to looking dumb

on earth as it is

some of the things I like best
about myself I bought

my boots   my bright red coat
but other things   like tying a cherry

stem into a knot
with my tongue

I learned the old fashioned way
by getting used to looking dumb

on earth as it is

the sun still sets
speckled as a quail egg
& we are still pulled from bed
by a large blue hand
& we get to kiss & talk
together as friends
as the last cold days of winter
come to an end

on earth as it is

the sun still sets
speckled as a quail egg
& we are still pulled from bed
by a large blue hand
& we get to kiss & talk
together as friends
as the last cold days of winter
come to an end

on earth as it is

the hot young novelist explains
that they do not believe in the individual

which we read while eating an individually
wrapped piece of Laffy Taffy   we say
maybe I don't believe in the hot young novelist

but of course we do
we can see them right there

on earth as it is

the hot young novelist explains
that they do not believe in the individual

which we read while eating an individually
wrapped piece of Laffy Taffy   we say
maybe I don't believe in the hot young novelist

but of course we do
we can see them right there

on earth as it is

we are debating the calories
in a handful of nuts
while a check mark
of lost geese
tick themselves across the sky

if they notice our hunger
they pretend not to mind

on earth as it is

we are debating the calories
in a handful of nuts
while a check mark
of lost geese
tick themselves across the sky

if they notice our hunger
they pretend not to mind

on earth as it is

we buy a large bag of candy
named after the explosive tip of a missile

but since we love a taste test
we buy an additional bag of candy

named after the dangerous byproduct
of chemical manufacturing

we agree that the taste of war
is better or at the very least
seems to linger longer

on earth as it is

we buy a large bag of candy
named after the explosive tip of a missile

but since we love a taste test
we buy an additional bag of candy

named after the dangerous byproduct
of chemical manufacturing

we agree that the taste of war
is better or at the very least
seems to linger longer

on earth as it is

we repeat to ourselves
that *the long memory*
is the most radical idea
in America

on earth as it is

we repeat to ourselves
that *the long memory*
is the most radical idea
in America

on earth as it is

we love this world
its rot & ruin
& rumpelstiltskin

its tag-a-longs
& thong songs
& indigo buntings

but how can we tromp the
downtown promenade &
horseblind the suffering

on earth as it is

we love this world
its rot & ruin
& rumpelstiltskin

its tag-a-longs
& thong songs
& indigo buntings

but how can we tromp the
downtown promenade &
horseblind the suffering

on earth as it is

at some point the computer
notifications can no longer be snoozed

so that the only
options left

are *take action*

or *take all actions*

on earth as it is

at some point the computer
notifications can no longer be snoozed

so that the only
options left

are *take action*

or *take all actions*

on earth as it is

the succulent begins to pink
on the sill and still we don't know

if this means too much water
or not enough

but it's a season
for changing anyway

so I too turn pink
as an unripe plum

on earth as it is

the succulent begins to pink
on the sill and still we don't know

if this means too much water
or not enough

but it's a season
for changing anyway

so I too turn pink
as an unripe plum

on earth as it is

there is a song my people sing

when you are a star
they let you do it
you can do anything

on earth as it is

there is a song my people sing

when you are a star
they let you do it
you can do anything

on earth as it is

you've got to admit

the stars look
           about as bad
as it gets

on earth as it is

you've got to admit

the stars look
           about as bad
as it gets

on earth as it is

the makeshift protest sign
is pulled from the wall
at the discount furniture store

& as soon as we see it
we know

everything must go

on earth as it is

the makeshift protest sign
is pulled from the wall
at the discount furniture store

& as soon as we see it
we know

everything must go

Acknowledgments

This book would not exist without the support of the following organizations & reading series, where these poems found their first audiences. Poetry In the Park (Sandy Duffy, Lindsay Daigle, Sara Renger, and Franklin K.R. Cline), Woodland Pattern Book Center (Jenny Gropp, Laura Solomon, and Michael Wendt), the Be/Witched reading series & happening (Meg Wade, Maggie Wells, Dana Poole, & Richard Harper), and The Parachute Factory (Greg Lamer, Sarah Madison Brown, Rachel Moser, and Robin Lamer Rahija).

Acknowledgments

This book would not exist without the support of the following organizations & reading series where these poems found their first audiences. Poetry In the Park (Sandy Duffy, Lindsay Daigle, Sara Renger, and Franklin K.R. Cline), Woodland Pattern Book Center (Jenny Gropp, Laura Solomon, and Michael Wendt), the Be/Witched reading series & happening (Meg Wade, Maggie Wells, Dana Poole, & Richard Harper), and The Parachute Factory (Greg Lamer, Sarah Madison Brown, Rachel Moser, and Robin Lamer Rahija).

Mikey Swanberg is the author of Good Grief (Vegetarian Alcoholic Press), and *Zen and the art of bicycle delivery* (Rabbit Catastrophe Press). He lives in Chicago, IL and provides manuscript assistance to poets with this tattoo.

Mikey Swanberg is the author of Good Grief (Vegetarian Alcoholic Press), and *Zen and the art of bicycle delivery* (Rabbit Catastrophe Press). He lives in Chicago, IL and provides manuscript assistance to poets with this tattoo.

CPSIA information can be obtained
at www.ICGtesting.com
Printed in the USA
LVHW031028111221
705845LV00002B/75